By John Hugh Roberts
Illuminated by Leo Del Pasqua
Produced by Dale Bertrand

CHIEF FESTIVALS of the DRUIDS

Book Credits:

Original Manuscripts written by John Hugh Roberts

Production, Book Design & Intro Dale Bertrand

Illuminations/Borders Leo Del Pasqua

Book Designer, Intro, co- wrote Inner Merlin Quest
& Fellow Adventurer Della Burford

Photography Della & Dale

Azatlan Publishing
Chief Festival of the Druids
Illuminations
ISBN 9780987830296

Roberts Heritage Foundation
http://www.azatlan.com

Contact: Dale at azatlan@yahoo.com

Distribution: signed copies at www.azatlan.com
regular copies at www.amazon.com

The "Chief Festival of the Druids" was
written at the turn of the century
by John Hugh Roberts an Early
Canadian writer from Wales
The Illuminations for the series were
commissioned by Dale Bertrand
and done over a three year period
in the 1980's by Leo Del Pasqua.

John Hugh Roberts took part in many
Druid ceremonies as he was mentored in
these by the three women called the "Three
Mermaids". One such ceremony was the
"Feast of the Red Swords" or the "Red Stars".
It is moveable like Easter and aligned
with the full moon. He tells the background
story of the three brothers who were fishing
Hea, Hoa and Hua and there appeared
an immense number of fish and they were
led to a cave which led to a river on the
other side of the mountain and into a great
open ocean. This was called New Azatlan
and the feast he describes is still celebrated
to this day in Fiji and is called The Feast
of the Great of Balolo and in Britain it is
called Lampreys Feast. At this festival songs
were sung in ancient Cornish.

"Chief Festivals of the Druids"

The first on the list in respect to time, is "the Feast of the Red Swards" or the Red Stars — it is a movable feast like "Easter" it commemorates the first Covenant in Azatlan, which happened at the time of the full moon in the Sign Taurus (the Bull) and the Sun in Sign Scorpio (Scorpion) at the night flow of the waters (tide) three Brothers were fishing (Hea-Hoa-Hua) there appeared an immense number of fish, literaly filling the waters. having filled the Boat during the night the fish Sudenly disapeared. having followed the fish into a great Cave, they exeplored this Cave and came to a Subteranean River that Came out on the other side of the mountains into a great open Sea or ocean this was a great discovery inas much as the Surplus population could be disposed of in Colonies as they became too numerous to dwell in Azatlan hence was founded the Covenant of Azatlan, Same time Called the ever-lasting Covenant, (Iroquoi thal) the meaning of this word Stricktly is, Ex-tream. "as long as the Signs appear" the Chief Sign is the Bull (Bula-in the Kymrik) or Taurus. ♉. the Chief Star in this Sign is "Alde baran" (Bulls-eye) a Rudy Star, opposite to this Star in the heavens is the other Rudy Star "Antares" with the first is the full moon, and with the last the Sun, and mars the Rudy Planet.♂. is the Corespondant, or warior King, the movable star. allegoricaly the agent that executes the decrees of the three Kings (Orion) the three Stars Called the belt of orion, are also Called the three Kings representing three Tribes or nations in the Golden land or new Azatlan(Colonies) that is the Continent that then existed where now the Pacific ocean is— in the islands of that ocean at the present day this feast is yet observed at the Figi islands the appearence of these fish or worms that make their appearence only on two days in the year first in october erly and about the the end of Navember (between 20th and 25th of the month) they apear in Countless my-riads. for a few hours in the morning before the rising of the Sun, at the first appearence of the Sun they disappear and are not again seen untill the next year. they call this feast of the Great (in number) "Balolo" (Palolo viridis) in Britain this feast was Called "Gwil-Bwlala" but as these fish are not found in Britain the "Lampreys" or Sand eels is made to do duty, hence it is also called "Gwil-Lymrien" (Lamprey's feast) is it not a strange Coincidence, that the name of the Star Antares (Anti-Tarus) show be so in fact. Now this star Antares. is called <u>Andres</u>, in the Kymric.

Andres. (Seran Dres — Star of the Druids) *** + as a sign = 61.
or star of the South, while Aldebaran is the star of the north, and the
middle sign between these two is X or Arian. the sign where the Equi-
norial line crossed the Equator when this feast was first established —
this point is now advanced over five hours to the westward to X
The following is a litteral translation of the Song Sung at this festival in
Carnival about sixty years ago, from the ancient Cornish (Kymric)

When ruddy face Andres — Shall entertain "Sin,"
And "Sin" is Saluted — By Aldebaran
And "Nergal" the warrior — Be on guard at the door
The Druids and Christians — Shall meet on the Shore

1 = Sun or ⊙
2 = Moon or D
3 = the sign ♉
where the ⊕ or ☉
are at the feast.

Foot to Foot — Knee to knee
Breast to breast, embracing
With the Kis of good will
We will fullfill —
The ancient Custom of Lan——

4 = mars or ♂. Called the star of
that branch of the Druids called
Nergals. or Lords of Zeman.
5. Sand fish or eels that are like
eels. with a head like a Herring.

Now afloat upon the Sea — Between the Temple and the Star of the Ari.
Behold the Spirit light below us — Through the Crystal dome of Zeman &c
Those sacred Signs revealed this night.
We may read if we read them right.
All may sing the sacred Chant.
And make the signs upon the Sand,

6 = St Georges channel and
the Irish sea, under
which lays the ancient land
of Zeman. or Sachas.
* these two lines are sung in

Tra paror han anварwol i lanwr Kyurid vare &— Plurality
While the part immortal shall fill the pleasant Sea of Lang-
Where the Coral rocks are growing — In ancient Azatlan nuages
And the emerald sea Reflecting — Fair forms in Shadow land 7.8.9
Far below in fairy Grottos — Immortal Spirit dwell refers
There are famed the Drús and Kristos — The Sacred records tell to the
Azatlan city, first Cradolle of the gods Temple and records
Home of the Angels before the great floods
Hope of the christian, Faith of Hea-Dere
Resting at last in — Resting at last in — Resting at last in, the City of the Nér.

10.11. = Located in the Pacific ocean
15.16 = the heaven within

7

for the translation one verse is left out, this was never sung by the Christians, of a strictly orthodox class. but was never omitted by the Druids. — the purport of it was, that, they were the Sons, or descendands of the gods, of Teman. and expressing a hope or belife that this ancient land as well as the land of Arzettan would again rise above the Sea, and that the day of right, and Peace, and good will among men. Should dawne with the dawnfall of the churches, (Kooimp êr Egloorisan)

Now I have seen the statemnt, that the ancient Cornish language had ceased to be spoken for about a hundred years. but as a mater of fact I have heard it spoken as late as the year 1834. by at least a dozen people. they were for the most part elderly people however and non of them at the present day. are likely to be alive, I can yet remember some of these songs which I learned when a boy at these festivals. and I have seen the wonderfull Light that appears on only one night in the year, in a certain part of the Sea, which I have mentioned, and it is as different to the phosphoric light caused by a shale of fish in the sea as the light of the Sun is to that of the moon. or the Electric light to a candle light. I have also several times heard that wonderfull Song it Sounds as far away and yet perfectly distinct. and I have a strong impression yet on my mind of the wonderfull Grottos and the many forms that I beheld below the Sea. — I have been told that this must have been a delusion of the Senses! or a dream! or some trick playd on me! and when I asked why. "because the church does not admit. that god reveals himself in that way. to heathens!" — if such a thing did happen it must have been the work of the Devil!" — and thereby hangs a tale (tail) Kind reader, take my word for it. there was not the faintest Smell of Brimstone! draw your own conclusion — but speaking of tails reminds me of the astral Bear's Tail which cuts an important "figure" in these peculiar Ceremonies that I am now trying to explain to you.

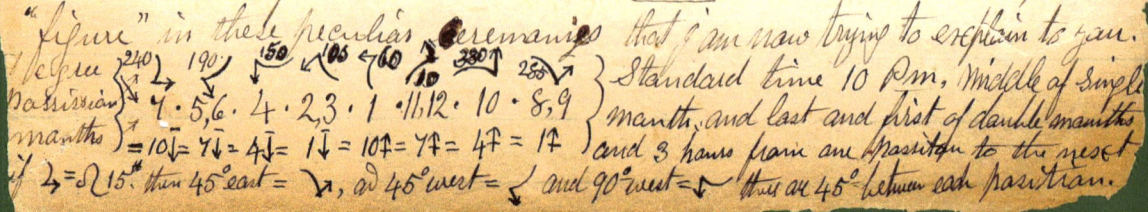

when Standing in a circle on the Sand, at the Sea Shore, each one of the company
watches the Master of Ceremony Standing faceing the Cardinal point, and
Drawing one of these Standard Sign of the times. So that all can See it plainly
all are requested to draw whatever Sign or figure which they thinke proper, — all
that are initiated Know the Complement required, by this very Simple act
the master can distinguise those that do not belong to the order of the Druids
and those that are, (even if they be perfect Strangers,) of the order. therefore
denids them, and addresses each Separate, and go through Certain Ceremonies
Suitable to each, then they move again and have games, Songs, and fun galore
this word gal-ore (ΓΑΛΩΡ,) gall-oor, means litterally a Gaelic-man, but
it has another meaning Alegoricaly, it is on record that when the English and
Welsh Started to the Conquest of Ireland that this Ceremony was performed by the
Soldiers on the Welsh Coast before they Sailed, because the Prophet Merlin had
predicted this, when he was in Ireland removing the Stones (which he afterwards
placed on Salisbury plains (Stonehange) because the Irish tried to Stop him
and those that was with him from removing the Stones — now I am perfectly aware
that the removing of these Stones is but a pure fable, yet I Know that there
is Contained in this fable, a fact, or truth, of far more value than any one
Could imagin that have no Knowledge of the "Kez" or the application
Merlin Knowing the Cycles of time Could have easly made the Prediction
as easly as he could Calculate an eclips or the age of the moon at any time.
the following words are the conclusion of this remarcable Ceremony

$$´7\,2\,0 - 9\,9\,3 - 3\,0\,1 - 4\,3\,4 - 5\,8\,6 - ´7\,5\,5.$$
$$ΗΛ´\quad ΙΣΦ\quad ΓΊΤ\quad ΝΦΗ\quad ΕΡΛ\quad \underline{ΑΞ4}$$

⟩ ´γ ··· ⟨´ · ··· ⟩
IΛ · ΝΑ ΓΕ.
yea · Nay

Êli — is the Guard (of) heaven the Sea rover (he that is banished — outlaw &c)
these words are repeated by the Master of Ceremony. and the Company Say
"yes" or "No" and this is entered in a book — then the triads are explained
and the first five Lines of the book of Generation (the Sacred Stone book)
is recit as follows, in three languages, which in English is as follows —
In the beginning were created the Gods, in the first heaven of the earth, And the earth
was without form and void, and darkness was upon the face of the deep,
And the power of the Gods moved the face of the waters, And there was light.
the last two lines are the Same as in the book of Genesis, observe the 2d triad 993,
is the year 1893 A.D. or 6606 of the Julian Period (the beginning of the end of the Covenant)

The first on the list in respect to time is 'The Feast of the Red Swords' or the Red Stars. It is a movable feast like Easter. It commemorates the first Covenant in Azatlan which happened at the time of the full moon in the Sign Taurus (the Bull) and the sun in Sign Scorpio (Scorpion) at the night flow of the waters (tide.) Three Brothers were fishing (Hea, Hoa & Hua)... There appeared an immense number of fish

literally filling the waters. Having filled the boat during the night, the fish suddenly disapeared. Having followed the fish into a great cave they explored this cave and came to a subteranean river that came out on the other side of the mountains into a great open sea or ocean

This was a great discovery, inasmuch as the surplus population could be disposed of in colonies as they became too numerous to dwell

IN AZATLAN

Hence was founded the Covenant of Azatlan, sometime called the everlasting covenant. (TRAGWITHAL) The meaning of this word strictly is EXTREAN. 'As long as the signs appear...' The chief sign is the BULL, ☿ ('Bwla'~in the Kymrik) or TAURUS. The chief star in this sign is 'Aldebaran' (Bull's eye) = a rudy star. Opposite to this star in the heavens is the other rudy star 'Antares'. With the first is the full moon, and with the last, the sun. And MARS ♂ the rudy planet is the cor-respondent, or warior-king,

☆ the movable star ~ allegorically, the agent that executes the decrees of the 3
kings, ORION

The three stars called the belt
of Orion are also called the 3
kings, representing three tribes
or nations in the Golden Land
or new Azatlan (Colonies)
that is, the continent that
then existed where now the
Pacific Ocean is.

In the islands of that ocean
at the present day, this
feast is yet observed.

At the Figi Islands the appearance of these fish or worms

that make their appearance only on two days of the year: first in October early, and about the end of November (between 20ᵗʰ & 25ᵗʰ of the month) they appear in countless myriads for a few hours in the morning before the rising of the sun.

At the first appearance of the sun they disappear and are not again seen untill the next year.

They call this feast of the Great (in number) 'Balolo': **PALOLO VIRIDIS:**

In Britain this feast was called

GWIL ~ BWLALA

But as these fish are not found in Britain, the 'Lampreys' or sand eels is made to do duty ~ hence it is also called

GWIL ~ LYMRIEN

Lampreys feast.

Is it not a strange co~incidence that the name of the star Antares (Anti~Tarus) should be so in fact? Now this star Antares is called Andres in the Kymrih:

2.   An ~ dres   1.

Seran ~ Dres: Star of the Druids

as a sign = 61 ,

OR STAR OF THE SOUTH, while Aldebaran is the star of the north, and the middle sign between these two is

OR Orion, the sign where the equinoxial line crossed the Equator when this feast was first established. This point is now advanced over five hours to the westward, to:

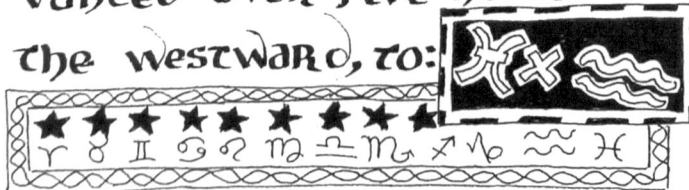

The following is
a literal translation
of the song sung at this
festival in Cornwall
about sixty years ago,
from the ancient Cornish
(Kymric)...

When Rudy face Andres shall entertain "San",[1]
And "Sin",[2] is saluted by Alderbaran,[3]
And "Nergal",[4] the warrior Be on guard at the door
The Druids & Christians Shall meet on the shore
Foot to foot ~ knee to knee
Breast to breast embracing

☆ ☆ ☆ ☆ ☆ ☆ ☆ ☆ ☆ ☆ ☆

1. Sun or ☉.   2. Moon or ☽.

3. The sign ♉ where the ⊕ or ☺ are at the feast.

4. Mars or ♂ called the star of that branch of the Druids called NERGALS or LORDS OF TAMAN.

ith the kis of good~
will
e will fullfill~
he ancient custom
of Lamprying.[5]

ow afloat upon the sea~[6]
etween the Temple[7]
and the star of the Drl~
ehold the Spirit light
below us~
hrough the Crystal dome
of Teman[8]
hose sacred[9] signs revealed
this night,

* ☆ ☆ ☆ ☆ * *

[5] Sand fish or eels. These are like
eels, with a head like a herring.

[6] St George's Channel on the Irish
Sea, under which lays the ancient
land of TEMAN or SAHAS.

[7], [8], [9] refers to the Temple & records.

We may read if we read them right,
All may sing the sacred Chant,
And make the signs upon the sand,
Tra paro'r rhan anvarwol i lanw'r hyvrid vore *
While the part immortal shall fill the pleasant sea*
Where the coral rocks are growing, ~ in ancient
✳ AZATLAD ✳ 10.
And the emerald sea reflecting their forms in shadowland 11.
Far below in fairy grottos immortal spirits dwell
There are found the Drus 12.
& Kristos 13. ~ the sacred records tell.

☆ ☆ ☆ ☆ ☆ ☆ ☆

** These two lines are sung in plurality of languages.
10, 11. = Located in the Pacific Ocean.

21

AZATLAN CITY

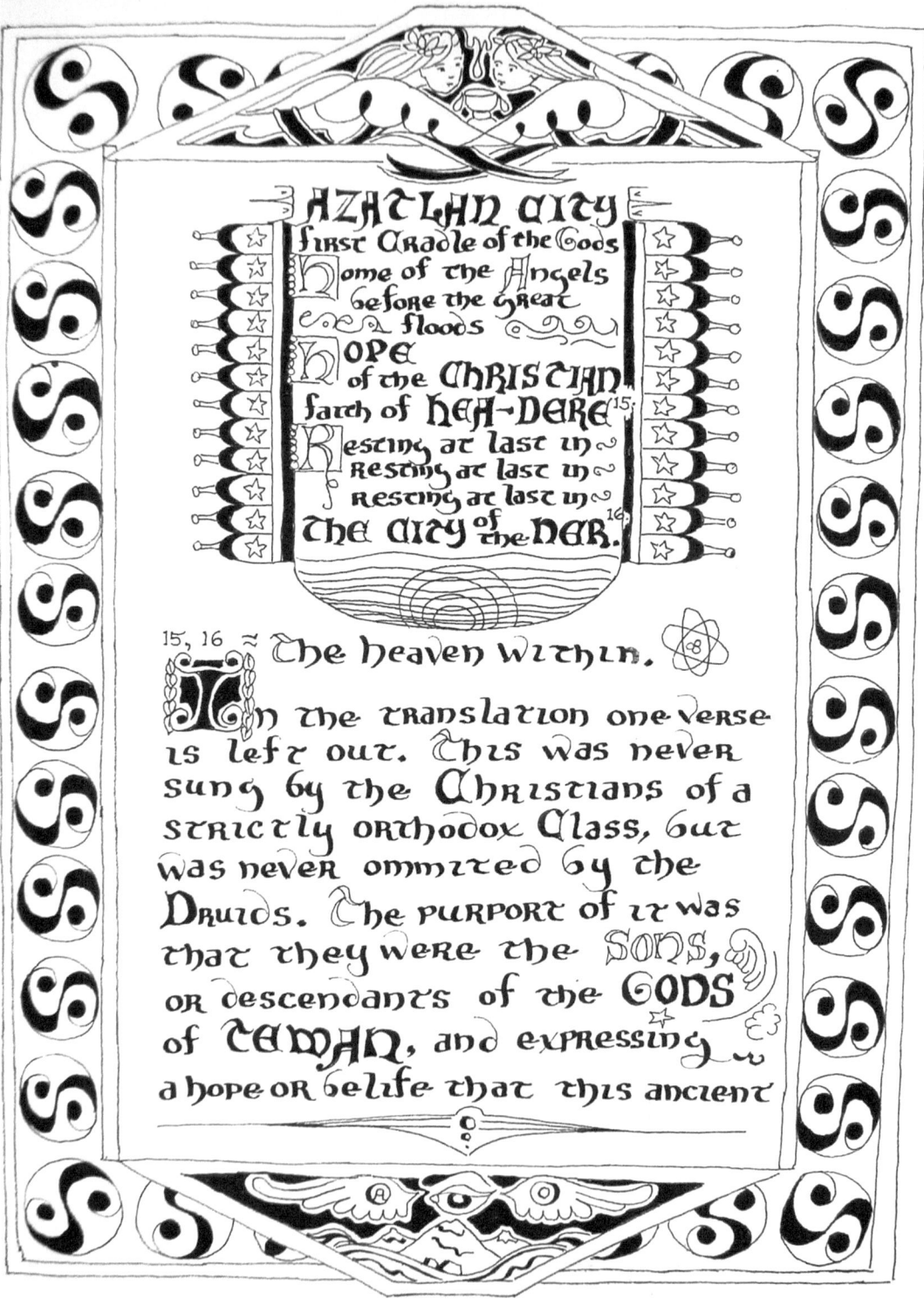

First Cradle of the Gods
Home of the Angels
before the Great
floods
HOPE
of the CHRISTIAN
faith of HEA-DERE [15]
Resting at last in
Resting at last in
Resting at last in
THE CITY of the NER. [16]

15, 16 ≈ The heaven within.

In the translation one verse
is left out. This was never
sung by the Christians of a
strictly orthodox Class, but
was never ommited by the
Druids. The purport of it was
that they were the SONS,
or descendants of the GODS
of TEWAN, and expressing
a hope or belife that this ancient

land, as well as the land of AZATLAN would again rise above the sea, and that the day of right and Peace and goodwill among men should dawne with the downfall of the Churches (KOOIMP ÊR EGLOOISIAU).

Now I have seen the state-ment that the ancient Cornish language had ceased to be spoken for about a hun-dred years, but as a mater of fact I have heard it spoken as late as the year 1834 by at least a dozen people. They were for the most part elderly people, however, and none of them at the present day are likely to be alive.

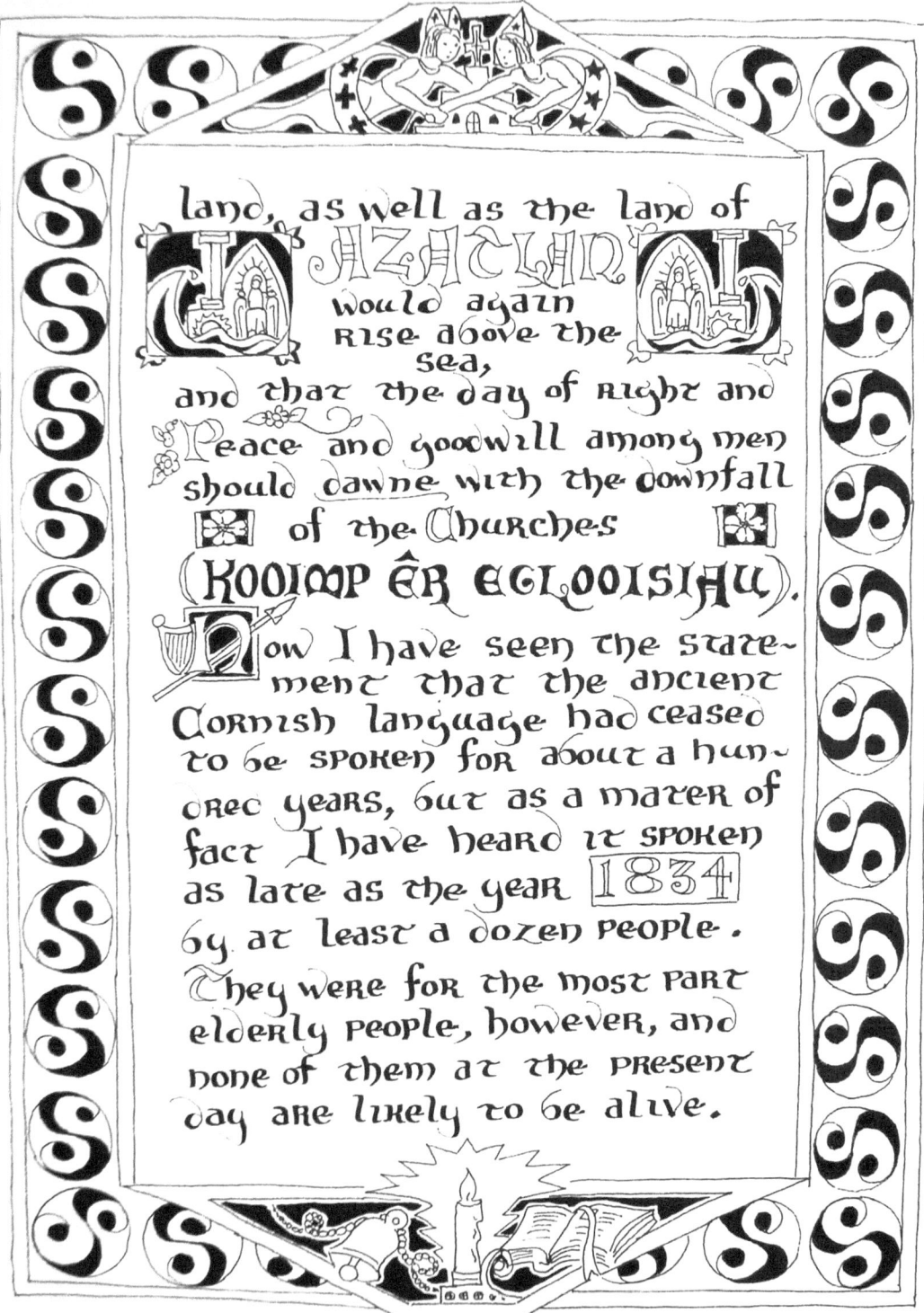

 can yet remember some of those songs which I learned when a boy at these festivals, and I have seen the wonderfull Light that appears on only one night in the year, in a certain part of the sea, which I have mentioned And it is as different to the phosphoric light caused by a shale of fish in the sea as the light of the sun is

 to that of the

moon,

or the Electric light to a candle light. I have also several times heard that

wonderfull song it sounds as far away and yet perfectly distinct, and I have a strong impression yet on my mind of the wonderfull grottos and the many farms that I beheld below the sea. I have been told that this must have been a delusion of the senses! Or a dream! Or some trick played on me! And when I asked why: "Because the church does not admit that GOD reveals himself in that way, to heathens! If such a thing did happen, it must have been the work of the DEVIL!"

And thereby hangs a tale (tail) kind reader. Take my word for it; there was not the faintest smell of

BRIMSTONE!

Draw your own conclusion ~ But speaking of tails reminds me of the astral-Bear's TAIL which cuts an important 'figure' in these peculiar ceremonies which I am now trying to explain to you.

Degree: 240 ↘ 190 ↘ 150 ↓ 105 ↙ 60 ← 10 ↖ 330 ↗ 285 ↗

Position: 7 · 5,6 · 4 · 2,3 · 1 · 11,12

Months: -10† - 7† - 4† - 1† - 10‡ - 7‡ - 4‡ - 1‡

Standard time, 10 P.M. Middle of single month, and last and first of double months, & 3 hours from one position to the next.

There are 45° between each position.

If ♃ = ♌ 15th, then 45° east = ↗ or 45° west = ↙, and 90° west = ↓

27

On this occasion the Riddle was 'OPQRSTU', a translation of which is given elsewhere. In this number I towards midnight, the dance of the FAIRIES is performed in three great circles, one within the other. When the sign equals 5, or 6, the outer ring disperses, that is, when the star ARIETIS

Ram

comes on the meridian, soon after one. The star ALDERBARAH is the signal for the second ring to disperse In another hour, between 2 & 3, Orion arrives on the meridian, when the Queen of the Fairies delivers an address, and the company disperses in five streams,

but it has another meaning alegorically It is on record that when the English & Welsh started to the conquest of Ireland, that this Ceremony was performed by the soldiers on the Welsh coast before they sailed, because the PROPHET MERLIN had predicted this when he was in IRELAND removing the stones which he afterwards placed on SALISBURY PLAINS

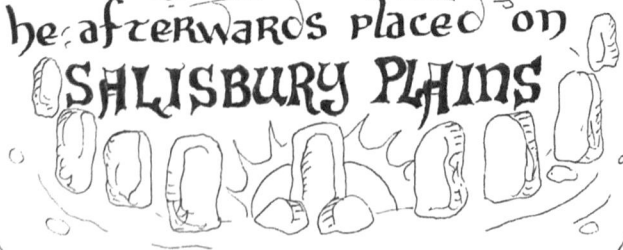

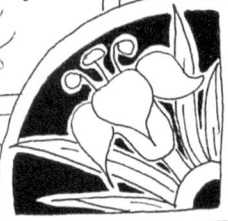

STONEHENGE

because the Irish tried to stop him and those that was with him, from removing the stones. Now I am perfectly aware that the removing of these stones is but a pure fable, yet I know that there is contained in this fable, a fact, or truth, of far more value than any one could imagin that have no knowledge of the 'Key', or the application. MERLIN knowing the Cycles of time,

could have easly made
the Prediction as easly
as he could calculate an
eclips or the age of
the moon at any time

The following words are
the conclusion of this
remarcable ceremony

⁊⁊⁊	⁊⁊⁊	⁊⁊⁊	⁊⁊⁊	⁊⁊⁊	⁊⁊⁊
720	993	301	437	586	155
HΛ'	IΣΦ	Γ'T	NΦH	EPΩ	AΞΨ
◖	◢	◣	◣	◣	◣

IA	NA	ΓE
yea		hay

ÊLÍ

is the guard (of) heaven
the SEA ROVER
he that is banished, etc.
These words are repeated
by the Master of Ceremony
and the Company say 'yes'
or 'No', and this is entered
in a book. Then the triads
are explained and the first
five lines of
the book of generation,
the SACRED STONE
BOOK

is read as follows, in the languages, which in English is as follows ~

In the beginning were created the GODS in the first heaven of the earth,

And the earth was without form, & void, & darkness was upon the face of the DEEP

And the power of the GODS moved the face of the waters

And there was LIGHT

The last two lines are the same as in the BOOK of GENESIS

Observe: the 2nd triad 993 is the year 1893 **A.D.** or 6606 of the Julian Period, (the beginning of the end of the **COVENANT**).

Spelling

When the papers were illuminated we decided in
keeping the integrity of the originals to do them
exactly as there are. .. even with spelling that
is different than we know it. Sometimes it
was done as John Hugh also spoke Welsh
or even for poetic reasons.

Chief Festival f the Druids

p. 12. warrior
p. 18 warrior
p.19 added picture
p. 22 purpose belief
p.23 dawn
p.29 arrives
p.30 allegorically
p. 32 eclipse

The Inner Merlin

Quest

"Inner Merlin Quest"

Dale's "Inner Merlin" Quest .. to listen to intuition, find knowledge and healing on life's journey. This mandala shows part of Dale's Inner Merlin Quest. Everyone has their own "Cosmic One" Quest in life's adventure.

Della has done a mandala showing the 'Druid Money' or Taleiferries (Arian Der) in the center, which is a connection to the cycles of nature. The three illuminated stories are shown -The "Mermaids" brings mentors, guides and friends to help and assist on the Quest. The "Gaelcerth" is at Samhain and is a reminder of identifying with natures cycles as is also done at Equinox and Solstice . The "Chief Festival of the Druids" also reminds us of the many sacred places in the world. Dale visited many sacred sites in the world to nurture his spirit, listen to his intuiton and find healing.

Climbing the Holy Mountain

After losing his hearing in his left ear, in 1979, Dale went to a healer, Rose Gladden and during a trance she was in, an Ancient Being came through her and told Dale would be involved in paths of healing. Minutes later he met and spent an hour with Professor Emeritius Dr. David Davies. Although in neither meeting did the subject of Druids come up but Dale had this sudden intense need to study Druidism. Days later visiting his mother he discovered that his mother had just inherited the Druid writings from the grandson of John Hugh Roberts. Dale took his "sacred ceremonial pipe" called the Eagle pipe and with his shaman's guidance went to Wales. Dr. David Davies suggested climbing Skirrid Fawr outside Abergavanny as a favorable place for a ceremony and Dale took his suggestion. David also shared with him that in a previous life he had been a Druid living on the mountain. He drove Dale to the bottom and when he left in his Morris Minor he raised his arm though the window and yelled out"Excalibur" . Thus began Dale's journey.

Druid Mandala 1998

Pipe ceremony - Kootenai Plains, Alberta, 1979

Skirrid Fawr 1983

The impossible can be a reality .. sticking to it!

Dale climbed another mountain which symbolized climbing and overcoming the frustations in life and reaching new heights - the mountain was Carn Fadryn, Llyn, Gwynedd. As he was climbing up the mountain it got windier and windier till he felt like he was almost being blown off the mountain. He knew at the top was a speical place as King Arthur was legended to of been there. Often in life too we go through struggles and after reaching the plateau we climb down knowing the impossible is possible.

The Ultimate Druid Library comes to Dale

Dale visited many places in Wales. He went to the village Llaniestyn where Roberts grandmother, one of the three mermaids lived. His grandmother and her two friends were called mermaids as their names had the sea in them. He also visited Aberdaron where boats go the Bardsey Island, to Carn Fadryn, Pwllheli, Sachas, Port Macoc, and to Criccieth where he met a remarkable man Jim Young who showed him a library he will never forget. Dale says in his diary- :

"... he lives in a beautiful house, one of 7 row house, 3 stories high that borders the beach in Criccieth that happens to look south over Sarn Badric and Black Rock Sands. He led me through the house and in nearly every room, lining the walls, bookcases were filled with gold embossed and leather bound books, the vast majority of them on the early Celts and Druids. My heart had goose bumps on it. He said he collected these books in Wales, often by the roadside when people threw them away during the late 40's and 50's. .. and over the years had amassed this wonderful collection. "

Below is another fascinating place on the LLyen Peninsula .. Port Neigwl which Dale feels is connected to the Nergals (branch of the Druids called Lords of Teman).

Stonehenge - and New Possibilities in our lives as well

John Hugh Roberts felt that one of the three mighty great works of Britain was Stonehenge .. the other two were the Ketti Stones and to bring together Klunair Guvangaon.

He went to Stonehenge in the 1840s. On Dale's Quest he traced his steps and went to the ancient monument. The miracle of how these were ever built and John Hugh's intuition that there were powers used by Merlin that we do not understand in the building of them opened up in him the idea of many new possibilities in our lives beyond what we believe and know to be true.

Finding Teman.. the Oracle was there and also within.

John Hugh Roberts speaks in his writings of an island occupied by a race of 'Giants of the Stones', where the 'Great Oracle of Teman' lived. There were 100 stone houses on the island and like Atlantis it sunk but the top of this island remained, now known as Bardsey Island, the 'Isle of Twenty Thousand Saints.'

Dale is photographing Bardsey Island below- where 20,000 saints are said to buried. The sea was very treacherous and the currents too strong to make the trip over. For Dale's inner quest to see Bardsey (even at a distance) and feel its energy was exhiliarating. He knew as he journeyed that inside himself he had answers to questions similiar to an Oracle .

Azatlan City - and finding the 'heaven within'.

'Azatlan City - first cradle of the gods", John Hugh Roberts speaks of Old Azatlan (Easter Island) and new Azatlan. We often wondered if the 'new' Azatlan was in Mexico as Roberts went there in the late 1840's with two friends to explore Central America.

Della and Dale decided to visit the island of Mexicaltitlan in Mexico when working there in 1998. The streets and all the buildings form a great mandala. As we search in life for the ideal paradise or heaven it seems that 'the heaven within' becomes more obvious.

To Honour the Seasons of Life

Many Stone Circles are positioned so they are aligned with the sun or moon at a special time of the year like the Equinox or Solstice.
How much sun we have in the world is connected to how well things grow and the harvest we receive.

On the "Druid Money" which Roberts has drawn as two mandalas the importance of the Sun and Moon's cycles is emphasized.

Dale visited many Stone Circles and Stone Pyramids that honored the cycles of nature. One he visited, Chitza Itza, was built to pay homage to the Spring Solstice after which plants start to bud again. Dale discovered connecting up to the Cycle of Nature is an incredible feeling of empowerment and can be particularly fulfilling if the whole community celebrates together.

Following our Intuition

When visiting Cornwall we were guided by Barbera Tremain, and stayed in the house of our friend, Sue Bladon. Barbara held the manuscripts of John Hugh Roberts and felt intuitively where we should go. We went to Cornwall with her on this intuitive journey which took us to the Nine Maidens Stone Circle, Zennor, Boscawen-Un, Merry Maidens, Carn Eunys, Lands End and the Mermaid Cove. It was fascinating to follow Barbara's journey and the lesson to be learned was in how to let things flow in a natural way and to be more intuitive in our lives.

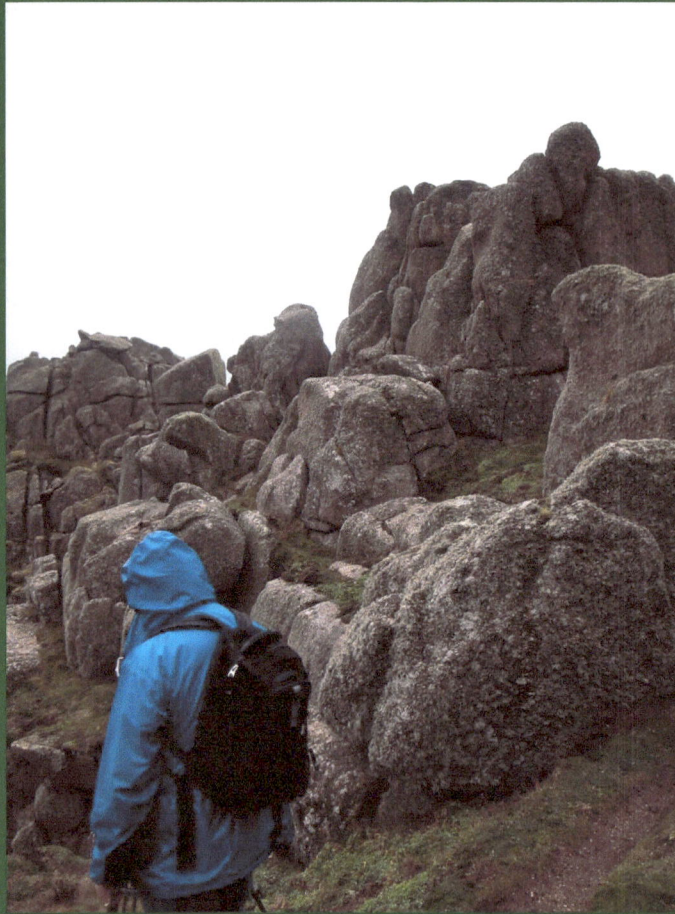

Healing Stone and Self Healing for oneself

    The Sacred Stone Circles can be places of healing. Below we found the stones at Bocsawen-Un very powerful and this felt like one of the main places John Hugh and the Mermaids would of held their ceremonies. One stone in the same area with a hole in the middle , the Men-a-Tol has been used in the past for healing rickets in children. Projections of the mind to self - heal oneself are ways of bringing the right energy for healing to take place.

The Magical and Miracles of Life.

   To connect with one's ancestry can give strength. Dale's family has strong Irish and Scottish backgrounds. He went to New Grange near Dublin and saw the 5,750 year old structure built to honor those who have departed and also show our connection to the cycles of life. On Winter Solstice a small opening where Dale is pointing to is where at sunrise the sun's rays come in and hits the deep interior, hitting the polished stone floor and illuminating the darkness inside the three burial chambers. A simulation was done of this and it was a magical and miraculous feeling of the sun bringing things back to life again. This experience reinforced that there are things magical and mystical that happen in nature and our life.

Sharing with the World

Dale visited the National Library at Aberystwyth and shared some of the manuscripts. They commented : "they were worth transcibing and analyzing fully. .. and that they knew of no other source which affords such a glimpse into the mind of someone who had "a zeal for recondite knowledge"

Dale is sharing the journey in understanding the Druid manuscipts and the 'Book of Knowledge'. He also leads workhops on Medicine Wheels and Finding your own unique "Inner Merlin" or Cosmic One.

John Hugh Roberts 1870-1917
This shows the family of John Hugh Roberts. His wife , Sarah, Missi and grandchildren. His son Tomhu Huron Roberts became a noted artist and at the bottom Charles Steele his grandson was the first boy registered as being born born in Vancouver -(1886). Charles passed the Druid writings to his friend Mary Bertrand .. Dale's mother.

The Roberts Heritage Foundation presents:

Vancouver–The First Years 1884–1917
Record by John Hugh Roberts Sketches & Paintings by Tomhu (Tomtu) Huron Roberts

John Hugh Roberts

Record Keeper/Writer –
In Vancouver from 1884 –1917

John Hugh Roberts was a prolific writer who wrote detailed diaries for 60 years of the life of his family. In looking at the diaries we can discover a lot about Vancouver. Roberts and his wife Anne were together for 60 years and their family of two daughters and a son were very close.

The Robert's Women and Girls– Anne-1828- 1922, Winnie (1882), Mary Miss Roberts (Sippi) 1857- 1932, Flossy 1895-, Sarah Anne Erie Roberts (Sis) 1855-

From the John Hugh diaries we get a lot of insight into the everyday to day lives of the Robert's women/girls. Their daughter Sis (Sarah), who was widowed twice, lived in Winnipeg but visited Vancouver occasionally.

There is many references to John Hugh's wife Anne in his diaries, and their daughter Mississippi (Sippi) who lived in Vancouver, and her daughter Flossie. Both sisters travelled a fair amount back and forth to Winnipeg, Toronto and Vancouver.

Part 3
Turn of the Century Women

One of the first Artists Registered in Vancouver- Focusing on his Vancouver period from 1884 –1917

Early Canadian Artist - Tomtu Huron Roberts was one of the early pioneer artists in Canada who painted the natural beauty of Canada. Contrary to reports of him being born in Wales, we know from his father's diaries he was born in 1859 in Collingwood and since he was born on the shore of Lake Huron was given the middle name Huron.

He entered the Real Estate and in 1908 opened a business on Pender Street West. He went to school at Mount Pleasant.
From John Hugh Roberts's diaries we read of many visits by his daughter Sippi and his grandson Charles Steele.

Charles Steele by Tomtu H. Roberts

Charles Steele's life - focusing on the years 1886-1917

Part 4
Charles Steele 1886– 1978 The First Registered Male Child of Vancouver

Charles Steele was the son of Mississippi & William, nephew of Tomtu, and grandson of John Hugh & Anne Roberts. He was born on Alexander Street in 1886 and as there was no registration office in Vancouver they had the birth recorded in New Westminster - the first to take place.
He was suppose to be called 'Vancouver' but his mother objected as felt it would be shortened to Van and would sound too Dutch.

His father worked for a while as a photographer and went in partnership with his brother in a photography company called Steele and Son Co. Ltd., in which Charles also apprenticed in 1904. Wonderful family portraits as well as records of Vancouver were taken. His father later worked at the Old Hasting Mill and then as locksmith in the old C.P.R. Roundhouse on False Creek. Because his father worked at the C.P.R. he got passes to travel, and

did so many times to Winnipeg and Toronto. John Hugh comments in his diary of 1904 "Charles E.H. Steele passed the examination for bookkeeper at Pitman College - first boy born in Vancouver after the life".

from Sketchbook Tomtu H. Roberts

50

John Hugh Roberts

Author - "Last Recorder of the Druids"
John Hugh Roberts was a Welshman who
lived both in Toronto and Vancouver Canada
from 1850 - 1917, with his wife, & family of 2
daughters and a son. He worked first as
tailor, and then bought, developed and sold
land. For sixty years he kept detailed journals of
his life. They had a house at Quebec & 10th
& then Point Grey. In his final years he wrote
the various stories and poems from his life
and "The Stone Book of Knowledge" He
indicates the information came from old
stone tablets in Wales. Scholars have
indicted these mysterious papers may of
originated from the akashic records. He was
writing these mysterious papers to to be
read by future generations.

Photo credit :Peter Gric

Dale Bertrand

Researcher , Producer and Adventurer

Dale is a lover of the mystical and magical in life. He has travelled extensively fulfilling his Druidical Quest for knowledge. Applying lessons he learned from his travels in other countries during the 70's and 80's he decided to follow his intuitions in decision making and very soon after this, synchronistical events started to happen which allowed an "Inner Merlin" Quest to flourish. Researching the Druid manuscripts and diaries by John Hugh Roberts, has taken him a dozen times to Wales, and also Ireland, Scotland, Cornwall and in following up on some of the more unusual leads to Peru, Guatemala, and Mexico. His inner journey and sharing the writings of a Druid at the turn of the century has resulted in 'Druidical Quest'. He has also produced various selected stories from John Hugh Robert's writings which have been illuminated by Leo Del Pasqua -- 'Three Mermaids', 'Gaelcerth of Halloween', 'Chief Festival of the Druids' and 'Nennius'. He is open to ideas for collabortions.

Leo Del Pasqua
Artist

Leo did all the wonderful illuminations of the Druidical Quest, and Illuminated Books. His art comes under many names such as Visionary or Conscious Art - he calls himself a Practicing Symbolist with a specific interest in contemporary Spiritual Art. He holds a Master's Degree in Theology from the University of Toronto. Examples of his artwork and poetry may be viewed at Urantia's "Brother Leo's corner" from Ottawa on line. Leo also has Ebays Veronicas Liturgical Art and is co-partner of a store which opens in the spring called "Getz Better in Old Killaloe" where some of his art is displayed.

Thanks!

Thanks to so many people for helping with this project over the thirty four years of development.
To John Hugh Roberts for his inspirational work.
Dr. David Davies for his integrity and motivation. Della for her motivation, perseverance and especially for her love. Everil Helweg Larson-Young & Dr. Henryk Binder for their wisdom and sense of adventure. Doug Atkins for his eagle eyes in finding the Stone Book of Knowledge. Mary Bertrand for her love and instilling the love of "history". Jim Young for saving so many important books in the 40's and 50's from destruction. Leo Del Pasqua for his wonderful illuminations. Bill & Patricia Meilan for sharing many mysteries and for his poetry and both for their love of Wales. Stevanne for support. Cayo Evans for his love of Wales and his great Welsh hospitality. Shanti (John) Baldwin for his transcriptions and friendship. Dr. Jordan Paper for co-journeying to magical North Wales, etc. Elwyn Roberts and Marian Hall for sharing their home, and the adventure. Sue Bladon and Barbera Tremain for the Cornwall adventures. To all the Directors of the Roberts Heritage Foundation Mary Lynn Ogilvie, Edna Reti, Joanne Williams also Jules Atkins, Tom Williams and all the Williams family Michael, Pat, Diane, David, Loosie, Howard, Alice, Virgil, Bruce , Mark and Wallace. To Glen, Brenda and Rob, Laura and kids, Warren, Murray, Golda, Flora, Holly, Desiree and Norah and alll of the Burford family. Harri for helping the vision, To all family and friends. Sorry if we have forgotten someone. Thank you all so much.

www.ingramcontent.com/pod-product-compliance
Lightning Source LLC
LaVergne TN
LVHW072113070426
835510LV00002B/37